Katerina Anghelaki Rooke

Selected
POEMS

Katerina Anghelaki Rooke

Selected POEMS

Translated by
Manolis Aligizakis

libros libertad

Ekstasis Editions

Selection copyright © Katerina Anghelaki Rooke 2019
Translation copyright © Manolis Aligizakis 2019

Published in 2019 by:
Ekstasis Editions Canada Ltd.   Libros Libertad Publishing Ltd.
Box 8474, Main Postal Outlet   2244 154A Street
Victoria, B.C. V8W 3S1   Surrey, B.C. V4A 5S9

All rights reserved. No part of this book may be reproduced in any form without the written permission of the publisher, with the exception of brief passages in reviews. Any request for photocopying or other reproduction of any part of this book should be directed in writing to the publisher or to ACCESS: The Canadian Copyright Licensing Agency, One Yonge Street, Suite 800, Toronto, Ontario, Canada, M5E 1E5.

LIBRARY AND ARCHIVES CANADA CATALOGUING IN PUBLICATION

Title: Katerina Anghelaki Rooke : selected poems / translated by Manolis Aligizakis.
Other titles: Poems. Selections (2014). English
Names: Angelakē-Rouk, Katerina, author. | Manolis, 1947- translator.
Description: Translation of: Poiēsē, 1963-2011.
Identifiers: Canadiana (print) 20190152559 | Canadiana (ebook) 20190159499 | ISBN 9781926763521
   (softcover ; Libros Libertad) | ISBN 9781771713405 (softcover ; Ekstasis Editions) | ISBN
   9781771713412 (ebook)
Classification: LCC PA5612.N45 A2 2019 | DDC 889.1/34—dc23

Foreword

Katerina Anghelaki Rooke first appeared in the Hellenic Letters when she was only seventeen years old. Her godfather Nikos Kazantzakis presented her poem *Loneliness* to John Goudelis, editor of the literary magazine New Epoch, with the note, *"please include this poem in your next issue. It was written by a high school girl and it is the best poem I have ever read"* and this was her entrance into the world of literature, as she poignantly mentioned in various interviews she gave over the years. From then on she worked tirelessly writing poetry and translating poetry in a career that has lasted to this day.

Her work amounts to a sizable bibliography from poetry collections to translations, to articles and reviews she has written and still writes although time has left many scars which her delicate body shows quite eloquently; Katerina Anghelaki Rook has received many awards both in Hellas and abroad. Now at the dusk of her life she reflects on things she has experienced over the years and she has become philosophical. In an interview she gave recently she made reference to loneliness and how she deals with it. Truly *Loneliness* was the title of her first ever published poem and loneliness is the subject of her reflection. She considers herself quite familiar with the concept when characteristically she says that although loneliness appeared many times in her life it was something livable and something she lived with since she never felt alone in one place in life until she reached the unbearable loneliness of old age; and this she faces with her constant involvement, her graceful appearances in events which she always enriches with her sweet demeanor.

"The ravaging time, she wrote, inspires both the prose writer and the poet because with their work they get near the negative aspects of our lives: sadness, silence, survival, separation and the concept of future and most importantly the concept of Death". She has come to the conclusion that, "rejection means freedom" as she wrote in a dialogue between *beauty and ugliness* and this is the woman who attracted and still attracts all who come near her because of her internal beauty and her self-contention that overpowers everything else; "rejection means freedom since you don't have to fight in order to prove you possess certain value while you are ugly. When others reject us we feel happy because the fulfillment of our internal needs doesn't depend on them anymore. Therefore one can focus in themselves and discover emotion and joy in things others don't"

    Self-contention constitutes the basis in human happiness, a lesson I learned from this old lady, Katerina Anghelaki Rooke with the brilliant eyes and the sweetest smile. I met her at the Polis Art Café, in Athens, in September 2015 when I launched my latest two books and a common friend brought her to my event as an invited guest. She sat next to me at the head table and I was awed by the brilliance of her eyes, though she was a frail old lady; she even joked with me when once I mispronounced one word by placing the accent of the book title one syllable further from the proper one and quite pleasantly she tapped her fingers on my hand and corrected me. I was also awed when she browsed through my book EROTOKRITOS, an almost six hundred year old romantic-epic that consists of ten thousand fifteen syllable rhyming verses which I transcribed when I was only eleven years old in Athens during the summer and autumn of 1958. Going through the book she turned to me and while her eyes reflected on her endless sweetness she smiled and said, *congratulations Mr. Aligizakis this proves that from young age you were destined to become a poet*; needless to say that I floated among the clouds for the rest of the night. It was at that event when I asked for her permission to do this translation, which she graciously granted me.

~ Manolis Aligizakis, Cretan, translator.

Introduction

Katerina Anghelaki Rooke, glorifier of Eros and Life, was the daughter of lawyer Yiannis Anghelakis, a friend of Nikos Kazantzakis, and Eleni Stamati. She was born in Exarchia, Athens in 1939. She had her godfather, the great Cretan Kazantzakis, as her model. In her teens she discovered Cavafy, which influenced her in an unparalleled way. Her first publication was in 1956 with her poem *Loneliness*. Nikos Kazantzakis who introduced her to the Hellenic Letters wrote, *little chick of Parnassus, do not embarrass me,* and she not only did not embarrassed him but she surpassed all his expectations.

It seems that that *loneliness* sketched the great circle of her life as the poet. Similarly, her *conversation with loneliness* closes the interactive part of her last book: *Dialogue of the Opposites with the Merciless Time* as the loss of her 43-year-old mate, the British classical philologist Rodney Rooke, established her life relationship with *This tough companions*. In 2014 she was awarded the Great Literary Prize of Greece, the highest Literary Recognition of the country, for her untiring lifelong literary contribution.

Katerina Anghelaki Rooke represents, quite rightfully so, the second post Second World War generation of poets; her elegiac tone of poetry as well as her switch to more existential literary themes, later on in life, such as the devastating effects of time on a human life, the inevitability of death and the routine patterns of everyday life bear witnesses to her establishment as a people's poet.

Her poetry, explicitly erotic and passionate, defines her sensual relationship with the world, such a poet of passion, though over time Katerina Anghelaki-Rooke became more thoughtful, paying attention to memory and to the chthonian and heavenly sense of a world that never loses its primeval powers. Equally dedicated is her intensity when she deals with her place of birth with its fluidity and music that transcend her poetry thus making it timeless and eternal; Katerina's poetry remains eternally dedicated to a natural element as well as to the beauty and the pain life creates, the committee decided unanimously when they awarded her with the highest prize of the Hellenic Letters.

Katerina Anghelaki Rooke is lead to the eternal through her embodiment of pain and transformation of it into a unique body that while it exists it embraces decay and therefore it transcends mortality. Yet what are the key elements that define this poet, the spiritual heir of the one and only Nikos Kazantzakis? As she said in an interview, *poetry can become a shadow. Growing under the shadow of such a tall spiritual tree is not easy; somewhere, something will affect one; and I grew up under the imposing figure of Kazantzakis, as we exchanged numerous letters over time, since I remember I met him for the last time when I was seven years old.*

For Katerina poetry and life are aligned. One can't be one without the other. *The substratum of the poem is the wound, the suffering, while the poem becomes the quest for healing, for the cure.* Although she doesn't remember why she wrote her first poem at the tender age of 14, yet she recalls her first composition:

> *The stars, the stars/ how they shine/flowerbeds of the garden// in the fresh morning/like a colorless good-bye /of good people who are away.*

The issues of health she has faced have played a decisive role in shaping her work, as she admits in many of her interviews. The body becomes her central pillar, her most important poetic subject, which is revealed in innumerable places in her poetry collections. The body is experienced in its material and spiritual essence mainly through love, as evidenced by the words *body* and *love* which also appear in titles of poems as well as books. Some of them are: *The Beautiful Desert of the Flesh, The Matter Only, Anorexia of Existence, When the Body* and others.

It is important to mention how various scholars and reviewers tried to divide her work in various periods: In the first period where the abstract symbols and mythological elements dominate; in the second period where the poet moves into a more specific localization of pain and suffering in a more earthy style and to her sense of the physical body. Here she restricts the use of the myth, as she writes about herself trying to find solace and liberation from issues of guilt and uneasiness. And finally, in the 3rd period, where the poet expresses an intense metaphysical anxiety, dealing with existential issues without, however, falling into sentiment and simplicity. Gradually as she progresses into her poetic path, we discover a universal, deeply humanistic style of poetry where from the personal experiences we move on to collective.

The art of poetry transforms sorrow into creation; it becomes that redeeming path which leads the poet and reader from decay to regeneration, from the space of sorrow to the glorious way of love and life and truly Katerina writes that she has managed to turn *the end of life (death) into Eros"*. Katerina's work undoubtedly reads as optimistic poetry with elements of nostalgia and melancholy when she contemplates on the human condition. Poetry for her is that centripetal force that defines its center of gravity of her poetic soul. And if the centrifugal force of loss and pain lead her to escape from her circular orbit, from her peaceful demeanor, poetry does not let her get crushed. It becomes the core of her existence, the sailing salvation of her life, a component of her psychic power that is applied through her fingers, creating poetry and defining her much-needed inspiration. Eros, the tiny, winged God, is the invincible force that stands opposite the devastating time and with poetry as its vehicle manifests redemption. In her *Existential Questions and Answers* she writes:

> *How beautiful Eros was/Eros, the opposite of truth/gave substance to reality.*

In conclusion, there can't be existence without future. Plato's love that exists in everything thrives in the field of Plato as she writes:

> *How does being exist without future/When only an idea leads to the body/does the dream alone bring passion?/As far as Eros is concerned, the last one/is as intense as the first one:/it grows in Plato's field.*

For Katerina Angelaki Rouke life without Eros ceases to have value, life without the sperm of love is tantamount to death. In fact, she confesses, *No life is stronger than desire, no act more complete than poetry.* Truly love guards her life and transforms her pain into poetry, each of her wounds into a miracle. *Love from being longing and passion has become a good friend that now enjoys the melancholy of passing time* while poetry, this highest form of art, can portray infinity because it makes her *forget the closed horizon of her future* as she walks towards immortality.

~ Chrysa Nikolaki
Theologist, Poet, Writer, Literary critic (Master of Arts, Hellenic Open University)

Contents

FOREWORD by the Translator ... 5
INTRODUCTION by Chrysa Nikolaki ... 7

WOLVES AND CLOUDS
   The Vitos Calendar
      First Day ... 15
      Second Day ... 16
      Third Day ... 17
      Fourth Day ... 18
      Sixth Day ... 19
      Ninth Day ... 20

POEMS 1963-1969
   Sleep and Dawn in this Land ... 23
   Erotic Poems After Death ... 33
   Three Poems About Sorrow ... 38

THE SCATTERED PAPERS OF PENELOPE
   Penelope Says ... 43
   On Earth ... 45
   Where I Was Born One Could Lose Everything ... 47
   Winter the Teacher ... 48
   Time for a Person in Love ... 49
   Last Light ... 50

ADVERSE EROS
   In the Forest ... 53
   I Have a Stone ... 55
   Heat ... 56
   The Cicada ... 57
   The Fountain ... 58
   Writing ... 59
   Season for a Fall ... 60
   Helen ... 61

EMPTY NATURE
   Oestrus for Death ... 65
   Three Poems of the Heart
      Heartache ... 72
      Place of the Heart ... 73

    War Calendar   74
THE BEAUTIFUL DESERT OF THE FLESH
    The Wind Perked Up   85
    The Source of Tears   86
    The Plain   87
    The Transliteration of Nightmare   88
    The Initiate   89
    It Appeared in Other Poems Too   92
ONLY THE MATTER
    Only the Matter   95
    Antediluvian Oestrus   96
TRANSLATING THE END OF LIFE INTO EROS
    Translating the End of Life into Eros   103
    The Term Sky   104
    Shape and Contents of Hope   105
    Secrets of the Profession   106
    Recipe for Life   107
    Atmospheric Poetry   108
ANOREXIA OF EXISTENCE
    Existential Questions and Answers   111
    The Goddess Habit   112
    What Poetry Gives, What It Takes   114
    The Moon Vanishes Too   115
    Simple Bed   116
    Unexpected Development   117
    Alienation of Attraction   118
    The Blessing of Absence   119
    Nature with One Meaning   120
    Stowaway in a Dream   121
    The Causality of Tears   122
    Season of Antipathy   123
    Total Destruction of the Ego   125
    Life Saving Details   126
    Reminders of Eros   127
    Poetic Postscript   128

The Poet   129
The Translator   131

Wolves and Clouds
(1963)

The Vitos Calendar
To the memory of Nikos Kazantzakis

FIRST DAY

My body became the beginning of a voyage.

Lights on the shore, a funeral procession
for the verdure of summer
the calls of mothers
took an autumnal echo
in the forgiveness of twilight.

I walk as the first rain
comes from the sea
for me the escape — quench of
an ancient thirst — was called death.

May the soft winds blow
and slowly mark the orchards of the horizon
that we, the final comrades, shall cultivate.
Silent caiques await the morning twilight
in the nightly quietness of the harbor.

The taste of the grape and of the fig
belong to memory now.

My body became the beginning of a voyage.

SECOND DAY

There is not a separating line between
the light of day and the light of night.
The hull and the revelry of the prow
squeak the continuance of endlessness.
My soul, the fiery whirlwind,
promises nothing.

I who dreamed of landscapes
where horses galloped unimpeded
in slippery paths of sun-downs
I envisioned my body in heights
in armories and pulpits.
Yet I often ended my days
at the ancestral well where
faces and things of the yard remained
with me for many forgotten years.

The beauty of the mountain vanishes
if you don't have a vantage point
from where to gaze.
I assumed the role of the cloud
which won't ever bring a blessing.

THIRD DAY

September noon
small talk of the comrades
in the gentle sunshine.
The afternoon colors prepare
autumnal steps.
The joy of my fate: death
peace is the miracle
that mercilessly precedes.

FOURTH DAY

Pale faces of trees
vaguely visible in light sleep
plain wind without
the message of the acacia.

The seven girls
close their necks to fear
afraid of the light, the rain
that their unlearned hands
won't get wild of the salinity.
They wave goodbye
to their names and hair.

SIXTH DAY

Your face extended
like the whitewashed rooms
of the paternal home.
The doves were taking communion
from your hand and they were leaving
in your eyes compassion for
the crawlers and little earth beings.
Your high-noon bloomed like carnation
and you saunter among the tall columns
decorating them under the night stars.

Now you lean on pride
the altar of sighs

NINTH DAY

We were making plans for
our death tonight
and it was as if guessing
the songs along with the fishermen
distancing themselves from the shore.

The glance of the sun might be bold
or would the roots of ancient trees
enclose ever tightly
or would we sink in endless waters
with the weight of the days?

Metal clatter and chirps
of wounded birds high up in the air
sea made of wheat
or would we die
of the many sunflowers?

Poems 1963-1969
(1971)

Sleep and Dawn in this Land

I

Oh Greece
the full moon pushes you
toward dawn
the tree tops move their shadows
the soft palm of the wind
maintains serenity over the sea.

Oh Greece
after the oil lamb is put out
you're measured
by the flowers of the dusk
by the stones
although some say that
as they're motionless
they symbolize death.

II

I walked from the harbor
to the house so many times!
After church service
one turns and always
something obstructs his breath
the moon or the wind
or a small shrub that stirs.
From the harbor to the house
madam Xanthi died
the ten, eighteen year old
kore vanished
the old house of the crazy woman fell in.
The familiar magical landscape
toward the field
spreads inside me during night.

Acceptance and revolution
always start on my soil.

III

The crop of September;
rosy rinds hold up the house
among the thousand deaths
they hold it up
while the untouchable moon
passes over our dreams.
In such concern I didn't notice
the small worm
by the spring behind the eucalyptus;
the small worm, the devil's tool
behind the mountain
small insignificant it slid
down from the cloud to the shrub
and bit the leaf...
we lost the crop, we the ignorant
in the balcony, were foreseeing
the crop of the house,
oh Greece, the next morning
I found you changed.

IV

On her bed the girl faces the wall
she plays with the worn out stucco
she draws
sometimes a person's face
sometimes a ship
that foretells the future
a fairy with the seven fingers dances
the serpent, the old nail
tie the tale together.
Turned to the wall
she befriends an unknown person
she cries for a death,
always a sudden death,
mine, my mother's
and flowers, a lot of flowers
in the remote chapel by the rock
solemn promise to Alexander the Great
and to the other saints…
the dream, but a yellow wall
as the drawings talk to children
and frighten the adults.

V

The orchard moves in a circular way
around sleep
the gum tree and the cypress
touch erotically.
Mother becomes
a wet bag again
I walk in Paradise again
and I nestle up, nestle up
with the body
as if I were moistened soil.
Perhaps tonight I'll dream
of the world's end
the explosion of the sun
to its core
I know the meaning of
there is no hope
before I wake up.
Quietness… the dogs…
during the famine
father cut down the cypress
but he forgot that sin
in the plantation of the sky.

VI

How many times it dawned in Greece
before I was born
after my death
how many times the rosy color appeared
and the old woman with the vegetables
in the metro to the sea at Phaliro.
How many times Brallos
kept on being white
in the winter morning
stone different from other stone
first surprise, as I return
from abroad thirsty and
I haven't discovered the language
of my own things.
How many times
it was dawning in Greece
with the few, the small
the meagre
the bitter almond tree and the amaranth
with all the wrong things I learned
with everything I imprudently loved.
Dawn
I live here and I long
for this same landscape
as if I miss it
with each glance

VII

Something vague gave birth to me
even if they told me
I was born in the sunshine.
Small in passion and in sorrow
I walk toward something light
that will be life
and I stop…
I return…death.
I count time with what I've lived
and what is forthcoming
that resembles
the incomparable end.
Only, look, the craft and the fisherman
can't be separated from the blue

VIII

What time before dawn
I dream that I reach the precipice
and I fall, fall
without my body?
All deaths are staged here
by people
the breath of leaves is heard
new birds replace yesterday's
just to sing with
one flutter, one soul.
Where am I at that moment
the only important moment
that underlines the great adventure?
Where am I when
they take away from me
one spring every night
and I don't touch the womb
that gives birth to
the butterfly that dries up?
Ages!
All ages are poor
and the age of eighteen
is dimply lit by the other miracle;
ages don't taste darkness enough
and they don't count
the value of the body
the infinite nature of the body.
And innocence, like blindness
and the old fool saints
fly a kite up in the air.
At that time when the poets
match innocence with a wolf
that moment, known only to the body

that writhes, growls
the sleepy sky turns dark
I and you too die
a thousand times
before dawn.

IX

I and my ball are
the world
that fits around me perfectly.
I'm turning, I revolve
with the hours rayed on my body
I'm the beardless worm
hunched on the mulberry leaf
and out there, what a music!
Heavy door latch, heavy cloud
have shut me out
I feel numb, I stop talking
life flows thickly in my mouth
I choke.
I keep motionless
in the whirlwind of motion
I flow
I make the moment rot
in passion.

Erotic Poems After Death

I

The soil dares me erotically
from among the olive trees
and the weakness of wisdom supports me
during the full moon.
Whitish rock formations
images of decomposition haunt me
while deep wells
of knowledge open.
I saunter on country roads
where I'll always be dust;
oh, what silence among the bloomed flowers!
Passion intensifies
the fear of the body.

II

Greatness protects us both
with the sky's little lambs and bears
you, an adventure of the cloud
and I always here.
If we touch each other
I'll be the redemption of sickness
If I touch you
the beginning of the end.
And I remained
with the nocturne divided shape of the olive tree
with the darkness and the struggle
I remained close to the moss
on whatever pulls you down all the time.
I was left with half words
and I returned.

The old man will endure the night
nothing perfect has ever occurred
on time.

III

You showed me the landscape
and it was green and sweet.
It was a green hill
and a green tree
and behind them another hill
and another tree.

IV

I pass by flooded by the light
in the routine of the clouds
and suddenly I'm nailed on the soil;
a myopic ant gets close to me
leaves its burrow
its crumbles
climbs up from my nail
I'm in danger again
I'm again ready for death
with my belly, my arms;
I'm trapped
the ant wins
carries me, bitter, dried up matter
while the uneducated cicada
screams in all that passion.
Yes, the cicada
turns the day tangible again
short and contracted
but of such immenseness.
Day of the cypress and of the creaking door
my day
first thus simple
last thus simple.

V

October
and I became a shy animal
I discover wings I wrap myself
I find nests I hide
I winterize in humble grass
lately only my extremities shine
my fate has turned into
something deep and unbearable
uncertain, it touches me, then vanishes.
I don't know, ah, I don't know anymore
how all the rest live
how they survive among the clouds
vague images of passion
how the moon rose up
from the earth again
as the soil played the role of the Assumption.
They survive
with a dark seed inside them
a dark tree that grows
becomes the big and leafy
tree of fear and disappearance.
I'll die crawling
soft like a snail
moist, unconscious
my tough fleshy body
will stay behind with the cypresses.
You touched me and I forgot
in what decadence I'd stop existing
I who brought love
the seed and death
I, the fresh one, at dawn.

Three Poems About Sorrow

I

The spider and my life
but an erotic summary
sorrow of the leaf
small organism of nothing.
In each of my corners
a trapped lion
a desperate ant
an extreme shadow of light
and I'm even grayer
than yesterday.
I sweeten time
with a childish Heaven
till the day
one day
that I'll find courage
in death.

II

My time is
a waste of time
in nature.
I don't become younger
I don't age
nothing of my heart
touches the stars.

III

People who age resemble stones
less sculptured
more and more of faded color.
Passing among them
I get emotional as long as
I can help finish my day.
I pass, I hardly touch anything;
only the birds get startled
by the movement and
fly away to the blue.
I live compassionately
dreams give me shivers
I feel numb.
And all my plans
turn into reality
what little choice I have
when I think of all
the shapes spring takes
all the possibilities of my birth
such little imagination!

The Scattered Papers of Penelope
(1977)

Penelope Says

*And your absence teaches me
what art could not*
~ Daniel Weissbort

I didn't weave, I didn't knit
I started writing and erasing
under the weight of logos
since the internal pain obstructed
the writing of the perfect image.
And since absence is the point of my life,
absence from life,
tears and the natural anguish
of the deprived body appear on paper.

I erase, I rip, I strangle
the loud screams
where are you, come, I wait for you
this spring isn't like others
and I restart at dawn
with new birds and white bed-sheets
drying in the sunshine.
You will never be here
to water the flowers with the hose
that the old ceilings would drip
heavy from the rain
and my persona would be
dissolved in yours, quietly
autumnally;
your splendid heart,
splendid since I chose it,
will always be somewhere else
and with the words I'll sever
the threads that tie me
to a particular man
for who I long

until Odysseus becomes symbol
of nostalgia
and sails the seas
in everybody's mind.
I forget you daily, passionately
that you'll cleanse yourself of the sins
of sweetness and smell
and completely clean you'll enter
the realm of immortality.
This job is hard and joyless.
My only reward
is that I finally understand
what's human presence
what's absence
or how the ego functions
in such desolation, in such long time
that nothing stops the tomorrow
the body always renews itself
gets up and goes to bed
as if someone chops it
sometimes sick, sometimes in love
hoping that
what of the touch it looses
it gains in substance.

On Earth

Today I talk to the earth:
my good earth with the silent
black feathered birds of the night
and the talkative birds of the day
that live their lives
chatty, fondly
naturally indifferent
earth, you exist totally in what I know
of you, and the sky is yours too
and you'll spread yourself over me
like a soft blanket
with a few of my pictures
forgotten in the selves

talk to me, advise me, tell me

that as long as people live we shouldn't mourn them
even if they're missed from our side like water from the tongue
that as long as they live they exist in other natural beauties
they sleep, dream, taste fruits, fishes
they go to work, take care of their children.

Earth, you have sweetened me since my young age.
When they punished me
I turned toward the sea
and my heart rejoiced
send me your balsam again, strengthen me
to think of Eros
as if they narrated it to me
as if they explained
the meaning of pain to me, absence
and in your baptism font
I'll reimagine our bodies
glued together without anguish
him and I

like winged little beings
poured in nature
to loose in substance
and gain in love.

Where I Was Born One Could Lose Everything

In the place I was born one could
lose everything.
Time eats the words
and from inside the words
the ravaged eyes are spent
even the kisses
and the need to suffer.

Winter the Teacher

I won't make the slightest movement
since the teaching winter
has never stayed motionless
has never looked
inside me so sternly
with one of its gray eyes
and the white other
like the cat's.
I finally stand
the future shifts its numb foot
my other body parts
a simple mortgage of death.
Look, the room became
a night again
and the night a room.
Outside the void shines
in its white glory.

Time for a Person in Love

Time is different for a person in love;
one's not practical.
Moments come to an end with no results
future is planned with the most beautiful images
of yesterday's love
separation is regarded as death
when the feeling dies
one doesn't recognize oneself.
When we met at the grocery store
we greeted each other
then the dialogue started
euphoria of the first encounter:
if you had the chance to touch me
I'd leave feeling light and with
my eyes on the ground when the horrible
glance of separation appears again.
I let go of everything
the moment from the present
and I enter into a different
foggy and undividable moment.

Last Light

I was lost in there
where I dived to find you
and the prophet of my heart was speechless.
You exist in an absolute shape
unreachable even to life
a white spot
some cloudy water.
I want to exhaust my last light
there where nothing
stops the eye
without a swallow
with no self-deception.
When my heart stops beating
I'll still be alive
I'll be looking out to nature
I'll call you summer
with no memory anymore
I'll call you flower bud until
the myth pulls the curtain behind me
opposite the white wall
all are finished and white
and I a cockroach
someone has stepped on.

Adverse Eros
(1982)

For Timothy

But is there any comfort to be found?
Man is in love and loves what vanishes.
What more is there to say?

~ W.B. Yeats

In the Forest

I saw you among the leaves
in the waters
in the light of the leaves
in the leaves of the waters
in the reflection of the moon in the water
I saw you in the lakes, in waterfalls
in the lakes that light creates
in the waterfalls where light tumbles
light encircling your body.
You were coming out of the trees
walking, floating
over dewdrops
over smooth shining caresses
in the insubordinate black of the night…
ah, the night steams behind your shoulders
vapours on wings
and a mysterious triangle shines
on your chest: dazzling target
of beauty.
From the grassy areas to the hairy tops
high up to the crowns
of the superior branches
the highest frieze of lunacy
in nature
the voices of dead moths
the spring of springs
the unbearable bird of sorrow
I hear with your voice
that rises from the depths
where the bile and the soul
in one voice refuse to die.
Everything that's yours raves
in the thickets, in the grassy empires
of the dreams
in the glorious silence of the ivy

in the silent syncope of the fern
in the vinous fainting of the autumn leaves.
Your meaning gushes out:
that no life
is stronger than lust
no act more final
than poetry.
There where you touched me
where I flowered
where I almost died
from where I called you
adorning your *other* nature
there where I was crucified
where I suffered
for your fairy-like grace
there where Eros was light
but with heavy consequence for the water.
Untamed in the ruling of reality
tell me, how I might see you again
coming out to the opening of the trees
with your thin legs
wrapped in wisterias
with the sperm of birds
in the roots of your hair
you who brought the sky
for whom I spent hours gazing through the window
for whom the crows shifted their nests
you who spoke the words
that resembled wild marigolds on the hillside
you who shone: lips and words
you the superior being
of poetry in the creek.

I Have a Stone

I lick a stone. The pores of my tongue match the pores of the stone. My tongue dries up and travels to the other side of the stone that touches the soil and has some mold glued on it like blood. Suddenly my tongue becomes moist again; it moistens the stone which slides in my mouth.
I call this stone Oedipus, because like Oedipus the stone is irregular with deep gouges in the eyes. It too tumbles with swollen ankles. When it stays still it hides under it a fate, a serpent, my forgotten self.
I call this stone Oedipus because it has no meaning on its own it has the shape and weight of the choice.
So I name it and I lick it
to the end of my story
until I understand what choice means
until I understand what end means

Heat

In the heat of Greece
water gushed out of
our touching chests
I drank your sweat
in your kisses
and your ah,
in the shade of the shutters.
When the day progressed
to the wild high noon
you were aroused too
with your unravelled hair
your holy eyelids
your multisided laughter
in the salty prisms of passion.
In such an erotic peak
such motionlessness
only with the shadow
of our dark fate above us
the sketches of our beings
resembled an equation of insects.
August turned acidic
like an open wound
and the endless cicadas
again reminded us of the poet
at the end of the poem.
Sleeplessness.
The fly that intentionally defaces everything
landed on your penis
and savored your bodily fluids.
The watermelons seller
with his megaphone goes by.
High noon falls
on my legs
like a severed head.

The Cicada

A thousand summer songs hide inside me. I open my mouth and passionately try to put them in order. I sing lousy. Yet thanks to my song I differ from the bark of the branches and from the other voiceless natural speakers. My modest attire, gray and whitewash, blocks my sensuous furor and being separated from dazzling celebrations of time, I sing. I don't know of spring, Easter or violets. The only resurrection I know is when a little wind perks up to refresh the horrible heat of my life a little. Now, I stop yelling, or singing as people think, since the miracle of breeze inside me says a lot more than what I create so that I won't die of the heat.

The Fountain

In the moldy garden
water reflows from
the stony mouth of Poseidon
and the undefeated frog
gives birth to its new generation
over the solemn fossils.
Ah, yes sweetness unexpectedly
overflows the same way
the fountain rises again
among its watery suns
while my soul,
an unprepared squirrel,
shades itself with its tail.
And as the park becomes slowly alive
and the owls stir
in their dark offices
and the thunderous water dances
over the silent rocks
of the closed house
like a stately residence, my life
turns alive again
by the talkative waters
you pour in my mouth.

Writing

What a disgraceful gesture I do as I grab the pen while something stirs in the air: the skin of my nature. Like when late in the day he raised his arm and embraced me with a humble glory as his gurgling voice resembled a child's who recited a heroic poem before execution. His hand with the chewed nails was inserted inside me so that I'd become my own movement of internment; I finished each poem by staying in touch with it. I bring my desk and my papers to the new erogenous landscape. I start writing. I start the small engine. In the third verse the new inspiration has overwhelmed me. I suppose he's alive and that exhausts me. I start imaging more than what I do. My hands get sweaty. I put down the pen I wipe the three fingers that held it between my fat thighs. Creation is in full blast.

Season for a Fall

The gold of autumn
flooded our room
and your body stirred
inside me like the dry leaves
the children kick
returning from school.
Nature concentrated only
in one little tree
as it prepared its heroic
purple fall
and your movement appears
like the kisses of the wind
that turn the tree branches leafless
from the ego's useless decorations.
Ah, the announcement of the end
isn't as triumphant
until the sun rises
to momentarily lean
on the half-naked tree tops;
Eros is never so
sweet in the mouth
as I hold your flower
for how long? Just a little longer.
My revived body
was inoculated by asphodels
and impudently I long
for darkness, death
and the evil of the end.

Helen

The deep meaning of dreams is darkness; their images are explained by other dreams; the description of the lover is also an erotic event. A thought equals my other parallel life. Ezra Pound closes his eyes tight as if they prickle him. His poems get reborn and renewed in his silence. The world with its open mouth below you expects you to say that you love it before it consumes you. Then you put together a love story to protect yourself from the expanse landscape. Menelaus has also lived the drama of beauty as a loser. Dressed in his unstylish purple pants his penis floats like a fish in infected waters. No, it would have been better if he had created Helen himself even if she was just a poem.

Empty Nature
(1993)

*For Rodney
on our thirty years together*

Oestrus* for Death

*They turned the fear of death
into the oestrus of their lives*
          ~Andreas Empiricos

I

The spastic woman lost control
and the carriage bridled in pain like an animal
that dashed out screeching wildly.
Soon after
like sudden nausea
the memory of the real body
came back to her
and the unfortunate woman
restarted going on her small wheels
almost joyously.
Opposite, wrapped in the rosy hues
of the gray time,
the house where Thrush was born.
Ah, but first I have to describe
the reef to which I swam:
its shape, its khaki color
reminded me of a backpack
like those we filled with sandwiches
eons ago in our youth.
I kept on closing to the reef
helped by the waters
with their light-blue blouses
that had painted on them the cypresses
from the cemetery on the opposite shore.
The beautiful temptation had overtaken me:
to not ever return again
to close the underwater cycle
around my neck,
necklace of unimaginable value.

As I swam farther out
I slowly ripped the fabric of the sea
I kicked down loves that surfaced
I kicked them back to their weedy beds.
Then I questioned myself
if I had truly desired
those acceptable shapes
of the desirable, something
between the subjected body
and the empty talk.
Eros is the only godly glance
that might fall on us
the unbelievers, I would say.
Yet, look, how the sea with the blue
eyelids arouses me now
I'm lasciviously scared
and I float on ditch water
not knowing where it takes me
because I walk on
the invisible side of lust:
death.

---

oestrus — strong desire (metaphorically)

II

> *"...when their fear turns into desire"*
> ~ Dante, *Inferno,* Canto III, Verse 126

Groups of seagulls over the waves
gossip about the light
they comment about its failings
the worse of them all: night.
Something sweet, like syrup
is formed inside me
the fear of the black hole
over which I hang
like a little fly.
I hear prodding:
Come, come to dance
your limpid dance
on the slippery surfaces of nostalgia
come, come to say
the last little words
on how the internal was poured out
and the external ravaged the insides
abolishing the hierarchy
of the dreams.
Ah, what an inclination for Paradise this was!
as if a godly blue man
waited under the tree
as if you planned for a long voyage
with your finger on the map
like a poem that pops out warm
a passing god would know
how among all the tears
the inspiration of death
rises unimpeded.

III

Encircled by all the joys
she can't touch
she struggles with her paralyzed tongue
to at least sing about the olive tree.
And as far as the handsome boys
who turn red when they look at naked women
and all the possibilities of their free lifestyle
she wouldn't be able to sing a hymn for them
even if she was as talkative as a magpie.
You write poetry? She asks me
sighing as if with difficulty.
Yes, I say not daring
to admit to myself
that its unquestionably bitten shape
inspires me now
like its old beauty
when in a few hesitant seconds
it touched me.

IV

Decimated from all the magic spells
which proved to be wrong
I fall, I get injured and I climb.
My vase that contains blood and kidneys
falls, cracks and...
sh sh sh ... stop crying
and pay attention on how the body
of that man moves as it pours
its precious fragrance onto
the crevices of time
and look at how what
we call curls with a *c* to indicate
heaviness, how light
they fall on his forehead.

Although burnt up I retreat
trying to escape from the circle of his attraction
while the miracle in the middle
still dances to its future rhythm.

V

Finally, could it be
an unfamiliar mechanism
or shall we remember the beginning
as we return to the exit?
Perhaps like the water,
the soil, the sperm, necessary things,
which because of their exaggeration
might choke you,
you die
when your life becomes excessive?

The young man laughed,
and it was as if God,
in a moment of weakness,
had kept
all His promises.

VI

I listen to my life as if
it unfolds in the adjacent room.
I remember the closing door
when the space turns holy
by his fast breathing.
In front of me, below the little balcony
dead loves fill the sea
over which invisible pulleys
pull the islands over
the light-blue foreground of dawn.
For a moment, the night still
holds the muzzled day captive
and the house where Thrush was born
remains muffled on the ground.
Everything here that aroused us
will stay with their closed windows
with their foggy window panes-eyes
the dazzle that touched our skin.
Then the seed of Eros falls
in the poem and
everything is transformed;
the tiring quatrain
the gray weather
and the wheelchair of the disabled
woman that pants
climbing up to the stars.

Three Poems of the Heart

HEARTACHE

For Kiki Dimoula

Heartaches lift up
the structure of internal loneliness
with its heavy stones of dead passion
cornerstones of bereavement and
all other material of the stonemason time.
Each ache becomes an adult, matures
till it shyly reaches the one next to it
and they co-build the palace of suffering
with windows open to the old landscape
to the tree that feeds its birds
with silence and fire.

Heartaches have their hierarchy
when they put together
the prison of fleeting love
the fish tank of age
the bastion of mindless fear;
they work obeying the boss:
death and his helper sickness.
And they have almost finished their job!
The warehouse of lust is empty
the bank of logic has been robbed
the chest of absurd hope has been ravaged.
You can still hear
the crawl of the last touch
and the hammering of the last nail
before it's ready to be delivered to its owner:
the misery palazzo of survival
that all the heartaches
have put together
with such compassion.

PLACE OF THE HEART

For Maria Kyrtzakis

Don Giovani aroused the desire.
To what level? To what level?
Until with each new love its loss
becomes the only knowledge.
Sweet, sweet, I pronounce
as others say *worthy, worthy*
though him, drunk of all the shapes
of women he has hugged
pins me in his collection.
I was the emptiness of his emptiness
a body for his body
sometimes he shouted crazy words
sometimes his soothing silence wrapped around me
and I surrendered to an imbued nostalgia
for the place where Eros was born.
Because, if as they say,
our desires confirm
the magical place of their fulfilment
then the Desired One
is the only proof
that love was once
nourished in my viscera
like a hyena or a hierophant
one chance that was found
when man dared
to dream that he loses.
He presently loses his face
that he'll enter like poison,
like a creek, like a faint breeze
like blood inside the other man
and he'll vanish without
losing or winning anything.

War Calendar

13th DAY or ON LAND NOW

The heavenly fights descend to the ground
and Death returns to earth
the place of its origin.
Bright flashes accompany Him
the only luxury left to the corpses.
Truly, how evil has changed direction!
The actions of Death commenced down
in the mud, in the hooves of the animals
the boots, the bog, then He climbed
to the black clouds and into the innocent souls.
And now in the desert
that I imagine with innumerable
rosy and sandy breasts
that breathe as they near death,
secretive body
with its dark oasis hidden here and there
uncommitted, like spectator of perdition
He became a parachutist to conquer.
Now the progress of bloody flesh
exists from top to bottom.
The sky, a fiery past
that will be forgotten
and good will be established on earth,
it will be buried deep, very deep in memory.

14th DAY or ABOLISHING THE INTERNAL SELF

I am a grain of sand
carried away by black water.
The place was flooded and the border
between the two worlds vanished;
the internal world where memories sprouted
along with the weeds-fears, moss-hope
and the external world sunk in dirty effluents
of the last news report.
When the dam was destroyed?
Lava, sewage, feces
flood my insides unimpededly
my internal life has been quashed.
I decide to hold onto a twig of tenderness
to remember your birthday
years ago in a snowed up landscape
but your body weights heavy
over mine like so many dead
and those eyes of yours
were narrated to me by inconsolable mothers
their color, of a shivering lizard,
young girls with tears in their eyes
and wounded boys painted them for me.
How I got so plundered
without even leaving my room
and when I saw you going
the little garden of my sorrow
became burial site of many dead?
How I ended up as a devoted
spectator of the current horror
when I was only engaged in the skirmish
between visible and invisible?

15th DAY or THE LESSON

For Pedro Mateo

We decided to have another lesson today
as if not, as if not
all of us humans *powerless*
command of the people
or some *holy duty* that calls upon us.
The tongue, we would say,
eternal and playful!
What the word mascara means?
The extra face! How funny!
The words, small surprises
with their simple meaning, their complex duty.
However our laughter was stopped abruptly
thinking that even the tongue
talks in an absurd way these days.
Night has come, we turn on the light
and our dark glance becomes visible.
Reality graces us with the best lessons
and knowledge is firstly a heavy cloud
that crashes down on you
before it becomes light bed-sheet
that covers you.

16th DAY or END OF THE FACE

I was falling asleep
with my head full
of smoke of burnt up earth
while my heart was squeezed
by invisible pliers.
Though each night I imagine
the end of my face
like others pray
tonight I found on my pillow
the unimportance of my death
as a gift the war had sent to me.

17th DAY or ANOTHER ELEGY

Quietness on the first line today
only they didn't mention how many
scorched bodies they buried in the sand.
I wondered whether the desert
rejects corpses of foreigners
like our desolate bodies.
Twilight. I read letters from
the days between the two World Wars.
Pasternak, Rilke, Tsvetayeva
correspond with words and kiss each other
not knowing whether they'll ever meet.

18th DAY or NEW ORDER OF THINGS

I dreamed
that I was in the old erotic nest
but everything was changed.
Walls had tumbled down
new rooms had been built
whiter than lilies
with whitewashed nurses
who called me to go inside.
You know, I was coming here year after year
I was saying as if asking for forgiveness
while my eyes were licking the corner
where the mattress once was.
Now it resembles an eraser smudge
in a child's notebook
or the muzzle of a wild boar
hidden in the green mold
next to an ancient rock.
A bittersweet fragrance exhumed from it
that didn't remind of anything anymore
to the old woman laid on the bed.
The new order of things
I whispered as I woke up.

19th DAY or WHAT WE KNOW OF SLEEP

We don't have the basic
knowledge of sleep
the professor said on the TV program,
between two attacks in the Gulf,
and he added that the smaller the animal
the less they sleep.
Look at the bird
perched on the high branch
it knows
that if it falls asleep
numbed by the godly blue
it will lean downward
it will break the branch
and who knows into what abysmal
embrace of the dead it might fall
if it goes to deep sleep
if it deeply dreams
of heavens.

20th DAY or THE SHORT PHRASE

The sun resembles a mirror today
where its spots have moved
from its back side to the front
and a vague shape instead
of an idol stands in it.
The life giving content of verdure
the passionate expressions
and the beautiful decaying decorations
get tired at this time
that motionlessness resembles an animal
when it sniffs its last moment
while it doesn't know what
is the smell of the holy!
And suddenly in this existential soup
a short phrase rises to the surface
from the depths of the bog with the dreams.
An unexpected, forgotten, playful, childish phrase
with syllables unharmed by time
a short phrase, golden beetle,
came in through the window
phew, our new freedom!

The Beautiful Desert of the Flesh
(1996)

The Wind Perks Up

My friend laughed and suddenly he looked like my father
who would close his eyes tightly when he laughed
his shoulders would jolt and he would hold
together his hands as if clapping.
My friend, standing in front of the fireplace whispered:
The wind has perked up; we'll try to survive
and my father dived in his ashes again.
Reality locked itself
inside its present castle
raising the white flag of the unequivocal age
days of joy re-locked themselves in a few teardrops
something insignificant was coming through the air
something of an insignificant lust suddenly appeared in the room
something insignificant we said and life passed by.

The Source of Tears

What stirs me in images of the desert?
The light, as it falls there
free substance that no concept
can stop.
Its animals and a solid knowledge of survival
and the stars in a different dimension
silent windbags that fall
and transform the sand
into inerasable Fate.
Its males who are flowers with dark petals
wrapped in white and answering to choked names
females never existed there
except of the whirlwinds.
The eyes enter the cocoon of heat
and the last water shines
in a thought.
I enter where my shadow is born;
someone cool stands there.
That absentee touches me
tears flow
their source will never be my center.

The Plain

In the perfect sleeplessness of Eros
the thoughtful plain spreads in the rain;
its milky green water steams
its puddles growl
flooded by unacceptable passions.
The horizon is filled by foggy bell-towers,
touches her belly
together with the locked sky
perfect owner of the difficult
philosophy of haze:
the measured immenseness of the drenched soil
includes the silent agreement of beings
before death.

The Transliteration of Nightmare

To turn a nightmare into a poem
you need silence without crepitation
of the soul, of the heart or of the other organs
existing in inorganic chemistry.
Colors are allowed to dwell in silence
though the intense differences are prohibited:
black against the rosy
or the poly-hymned blue of the eyes.
Perhaps a little color of the soil
coppery of the wilted leaf
or white with brown dots from the neck of a dog.
After the nightmare grows tall as it should
it's subjected to a series of operations.
Its logical suspicion has to be removed
with delicate precision
and after that and without anesthesia
something has to be transplanted
from the natural compassion of man.
The most serious operation
is to detach horror from it.
You succeed in this when you constantly dip
the bad dream in the holiness of nature.
Then the poem sprouts:
little leaf by little leaf
flower after flower
sickly in the beginning and shivering
it sprouts up from the black soil
that nourished it
and dares to dream
the antidote of agony:
logos.

The Initiate

The initiate dressed in white always dwells in caves
and the oleanders behind him will turn red
the pebbles will be sprinkled with holy rain
and the whole gorge that follows.
I also go near with my serpent-self
the estuary of passion.
My soles, the last lovers,
carry me lightly
as if I had no heaviness in my consciousness.
The one who attracts me stops, thin,
dressed in white and having a ponytail;
he smells a strong odor like devil rosemary
while he exhumes the beautiful fragrance of a dead angel.
The leafage of the carob-tree
hides something quivering and invisible
felt only by that quivering and invisible sense
that we have inside us.
The initiate is very thin;
his pants only balloon a little
in the front and a little in the back
while airy flesh fills his shirt.
The sponsor of earth lowered me,
with the unanswered questions in my tongue,
to a cave that instead of a mouth
had a hole in the sky.
Under it stood
the provider of the inconceivable
who milked the light-blue
with his palms turned upwards.
He stirred a little;
was perhaps the unforeseen from above
that pushed him
or the earth, slave of precision
that shook him from his foundations?

He smiled with eyes-teeth made of steel
then I thought I had skipped
something very important before
time and day had given birth to me.
Firstly I asked about time
which passes quickly these days
with wings that only have time
to caress me, the wilted one.

When you're young, the translator
of the timeless explains to me,
you're by nature satiated
as if you gorge yourself
in an extra rich meal.
Full by an endless future
one hour seems as the whole feast
seasons have no end
eons separate fruits from snow
stodgy seconds sit heavy over the weeks.
Satiated by the endless time
the newly recruited body
won't get hungry anymore.
Truly how did they store so many
moments under the fresh skin?
Only later, when the storage facility
starts to empty of life
and fills with insecurity
what is five years, you might say,
I didn't even get their smell
while all along with more bulimia
you swallow the half-chewed mouth-fulls
from the leftovers of your time-portion.

We walked out of the cave
and I felt as reborn
as if made of stones and soil.
Half blessed and half punished
he wrapped my aged body with aroma.
Then I understood what I had skipped:
it doesn't relate to my birth
but to a death I hadn't mourned yet
a death that I hadn't died yet.

It Appeared in Other Poems Too

I never understood spring,
obvious in other poems too,
for this reason I have all the misunderstandings
regarding the flesh, hope
and self- knowledge through time.
I never manage to balance
the annual miracle
with the infinite silence;
the truth of the rejuvenated flower
with the one and only death.
Today I study again the new green
and the frosty wind being surprised
by the exhuming of nature
makes one step backward.
Light is pinned on half hidden peaks
and I find myself
out of place again.
The point is this:
the personal body
and its impersonal demise.

Only the Matter
(2001)

Only the Matter

I take something and place it somewhere else.
I don't know why perhaps I don't like something;
seconds later the cloth; then the paper
which screams a whisper
when its position is changed.
Does this imperceptible sound
perhaps expresses discomfort
or relief for this new relation
of the soulless to infinity?
Or perhaps the subject longs
for its old place?
A small imperceptible movement
a glance, a spark of light
and look, the internal-self springs out
and moves freely
in the abstract now.
Then something as an erotic murmur is heard
or a little whining of an unfed dog.
Matter will act as such, I say
before my own silence
takes control of me.

Antediluvian Oestrus*

A

Yesterday I was in a country
that I had never visited before
though it existed there all along
like a promise which mailed me
letters through the light.
I was listening to a singing voice,
a bit of a troubadour, a bit of a Greek,
and I entered the forest.
Ah, the forest with its houses
that resembled clogs!
Soon the little red riding hood
would appear and the evil wolf soon her,
I said, but the wolf wasn't as evil
and the grandmother hadn't vanished.
She organized festivities among
the celebratory leaves and indulged
in the life of a woman like a she-wolf.

Strong desire (metaphorically)

B

Look she said to me *the end*
is similar to the beginning
when the first and last trees are just a few
and from these you try to conceive the forest.
You don't know, or you forget, that Eugene
the hero is handsome because he wished to be
not because the heavenly
powers created him this way.
Standing straight up in the light-blue
he regretted complacently
that he violated his oath
he succumbed to his own beauty
and he hugged the squirrel.
The fairy tales, like love stories,
wander until they find the places
that best fits them
and Tom Thumb will seed
his destiny, hoping
to save himself from what
he left behind as his trace.

C

Here the stars gleam
like the fireworks-poems
flew up high and the earth deviously
slid toward the sea and looked
as if it never slept with a man.
Birds flew toward the warm South
and with their symmetrical shapes
reminded us of a forgotten alphabet.
Later the Ursa Major, old lady
with a lot of jewellery, came down
to the celebratory ball of earth.
None had anything to ask
off anyone
except for a little more life
and…yes…ah,
long as nature can
maintain its virginity.

D

Since it was a dark night
and only the stars flickered
I thought of an image
beyond humans.
The vase containing the sea was placed
at the edge of the visible
a few dark, undecorated Christmas trees
stood on the sand silently;
heavenly bodies
screamed and shone
in the freedom of lust.
The air smelled of unfamiliar flowers
and none of the lamps revealed
any true or faulty *present*.
Ah, yes, I said and pushed my inelegant
sole on the atrophied grass, this the way they were
before the stage of the cloud opened
to the first act, with the first actor
playing the first male role;
this was the way before they decided
to strangle the female babies
before Erasmus replaced our diction
before the first complain was heard
about life on this earth
this was the scene of existence
before the play with many acts commenced.

Translating the End of Life into Eros
(2003)

*For my husband
on our forty years together*

Translating the End of Life into Eros

Since I can't touch you
with my tongue
I transliterate my passion.
I can't take you as communion
for this I transcend you.
I can't undress you
and I dress you with imagination
of an allophone language.
I can't cuddle under your wings
and I fly around you turning
the pages of your vocabulary.
I want to know how you denude
yourself, how you are reborn
and for this I search for
your habits between your lines
the fruits you love
the smells you prefer
the girls you read as if turning pages.
I'll never see your nude signs
so I work hard on your adjectives
which I recite in an allophone language.
Yet my story becomes too old
my tome doesn't adorn any shelf
and now I imagine you leather-bound
in a foreigner's bookcase.
Since it was never allowed
to let myself in the nonsense of nostalgia
I write this poem and I read
the gray sky in a sunlit translation.

The Term Sky

Shrub or knife
am I laid down or am I active
is light unprecedented or old?
Walking up the stairs I admit
I don't know whether I go up or down.
Am I finding the answer
or total darkness?
Why we call this lust
and the other pain
since when the body gives in,
hanging or shivering,
does it know whether
it enjoys or bleeds
inexperienced as it is
before the future that will butcher it?

What does it mean to the sky
that the light descends now?
Since wherever you look
even in darkness
even into Hades
light exists there too.
Pain is an endless dark length
that you recognize since you don't
dream of light in there anymore.

Shape and Contents of Hope

For Kostas Giannakakos

Hope contains the dream,
the miracle.
Hope is conservative
like grandpa and grandma.
Hope is subversive
like the children.
Hope is generous:
some kind of life awaits for everyone.
Hope is self-centered:
let him die, so I can live.
Hope is natural:
without it
no one can breathe.
Hope is unnatural:
It makes you co-exist
next to the monster of survival.
Hope is abstract:
other than hunger
everything else is indefinable.
Hope is precise:
I expect this flower
dressed in this attire
with the light on its stem.

Towards the end
hope will get married to horror
and you'll hope and shiver
in the same breath
that you won't stay alive and suffer
or you won't give up on life.

Secrets of the Profession

As crafty as logos is
so it hides the secret of survival.
It hides between its lines
who wounded your heart
who dirtied your stars;
logos will become a false witness
that you'll regain
the reflection of love.
It organizes your defence
and your exoneration
since you sacrificed the secret
of immortality for a momentary
meeting in heavens, and
it makes you forget your daily diet
with an imaginative verse of a poem:
ephemeral, raw.
You announce with chosen antithesis:
I'm content with momentary poetry.
Leaving behind the loss
you search for new techniques
to hymn eyes and other eyes
for as long as yours remain open, you say:
I still have work to do.

Recipe for Life

I thin up the ancient horror
in dreams that last seconds
the daily panic
with a momentary heaven.
I systematically hate the excess:
let me miss the train, I say
but running carefully not to break
the water pitcher
with the little joy that has
remained in its bottom.
I don't betray the indignation
that more and more boils for something
though I loose
the defeat that appears
as victory and which
I place in the air to cool off
the way nature has coordinated.
I pass through the time machine
the murderous sorrow
of everything that I loved and is still alive
though they don't matter to me anymore
and I lightly dust with thickened sorrow
the evening meal
which life still serves.

Atmospheric Poetry

How many days of absence
the air needs
to get rid of the exhaling
of your skin
that the scent of jasmine or cypress
will establish again
all the beautiful fragrances
of the faceless nature?
How long it takes
for the landscape to maintain
that overpowering combination
of breeze and a certain footstep?
How long the cosmos will still remind us
the meeting of an unimportant glance?
When will the light regain
its absolute superiority
over the momentary triumph
of a human shadow?

Anorexia of Existence
(2011)

To the memory of Rodney Rooke

Existential Questions and Answers

How beautiful Eros was!
It conquered without guilt,
it fought without spears, without ambitions.
The high-noon became midnight
the ice turned into summer heat.
Eros: the opposite of truth
gave substance to reality.
The smell of sweat was beautiful
the conclusions of the flesh were wise;
flesh: the most neglected goddess.
Now I watch my life, a documentary
that rarely shows birds in nature
forgotten remote beaches
unreachable mountain peaks.
I watch the movements of my soul on the screen.
What method a soul follows to survive
a little longer without future?
The lie, the truth
or it lets itself in the nature of being?
Who's *being* is it?
How does *being* exist without future?
When only an idea leads to the body
does the dream alone bring passion?
As far as Eros is concerned, the last one
is as intense as the first one:
it grows in Plato's field.

The Goddess Habit

When the goddess Habit
protects you
it makes you bless
each small lethargic vegetable
since it makes your walk possible
on a path without a goal
without a starting point
since to commence on a path
you need to have a goal.
The goddess Habit creates
the dangerous balance
over the everyday void
and colors the empty
sunsets purple
as if by an amateur painter;
it does everything
with automatic movements
that make the days easy
and without any secret message.
The goddess Habit even
orders the breath in and out
of the lungs when everything
seems normal and only joy is missing.
I got used to it, I say and I mean
I forget in order to survive
I forget the body that is
wrapped in ideas and dreams.
And behold, the dawn comes
to crown my face,
ravaged by time,
with the miracle of life
that the poor tongue
can't name with any other
word but *light.*

Yes, goddess Habit
I believe in you and I serve you.
You too, stay loyal to me
until I get tired of you.

What Poetry Gives, What It Takes

What does poetry give and what does it take?
When under the weight of a cloud
all your viscera leans sideways
when one glance scratches old wounds
when a new handicap opens new wounds
when the sky's lanterns shine
at a close distance to your future
and when the pieces of life you've saved aren't enough
when a sorrow that hasn't yet come tyrannizes you
when pain has neither name nor color
then poetry touches your forehead like a soft hand
and convinces you of your special purpose
that your verse won't end with your life
that poetry is the accountability of your soul.
Then you take the pen
and you think of being one
with beauty and immortality.
But what sacrifice is poetry asking of you?
What does it want in return?
Only one thing:
don't demand anything
of the soil you walk on
don't expect reality to reward you
nor to enrich you
with infinite ties nor to become
the way you wish it to be.
You better crave for one thing:
that reality will remain around you and that
you'll love it being there
even if it is frowning, even if it is grumpy.

The Moon Vanishes Too

The moon, the moon
so attached to my breast,
to my belly; I don't look at it anymore
as I don't look in the mirror.
The foggy moon
lights faintly and only
reminds me of other moments
when along with its crescent
the full moon passion grew stronger
and you, wet on the pebbles
you thought you had captured
the meaning of creation;
you dreamed of a totally
metaphysical season
when the impressive sun
wouldn't stop the poem — moon
since the silvery light
is always more erotic
than the golden light of day.

You, foolish girl, thought
that you would wane
in the lascivious moon forever;
yet the moon also passes,
it too vanishes.

Simple Bed

How the movements leading
to a simple bed
can still inspire?
Bed without companion
without sweat
without impressions
an empty stretched bed-sheet
a screen without film
and movements meaning
only the end of day.
It seems I signed a peace
agreement without any battle
with no victors nor defeated.
Peace is only the sleep
that comes wrapped in
the hope of a dream.
Yet, quite unexpectedly
sweetness is spread over
the ravaged flesh.
This night is also over.
One more part of time
that I didn't betray
I didn't swear at the hour
nor at the moment.
The day was good
I didn't feel any new wound
nor did any of the old ones go septic.
A simple bed
with four legs
and summery bed-sheets
brutally white.

Unexpected Development

From which sky
does this poison drip
and moistens my life
drop by drop?
Where is that light
which flooded my life
when my glance fell on
his body, that was vaguely
discerned under the manly attire?
It was when words overflowed
images flew like wild birds
that refused to feed on words
even if they were hungry for them.
The night wasn't frightening
silent as it was, it narrated tales
it promised a dawn.
People weren't the tedious
opposite to loneliness
but wells that hid fresh and
consoling secrets in their depths.
I say: am I perhaps the reason
or darkness that opposes life
and comes steadily near me?

Alienation of Attraction

The flesh became page
the skin paper
the caress a vague concept
the body a new theory of the inexistent.
Truly, how can I describe nature
when it has abandoned me
and only in the premiere of autumn
it remembers to invite me sometimes?
I hope to find the courage
to express my last wish:
to see a naked male body
to remind myself and to carry
as my last image, the male body
that isn't flesh, but a future
substance beyond the flesh.
Because that is the meaning of lust:
to touch the perishable
and push death aside.

The Blessing of Absence

I feel obligated to absence:
what I miss protects me
from what I might lose;
all my abilities
that dried up in the infertile field of life
protect me from useless, tasteless
movements over the void.
What I miss teaches me
that what remains with me
disrupts my focus
since it projects for me
images from the past
as if they were promises for the future.
I can't, I don't dare
to imagine not even a passing angel
since I descend to another
planet without angels.
Love that was a passionate longing
turned into a good friend;
we taste the melancholy of time together.
Deprive me, I beg the Unknown,
deprive me a little more
that I'll survive.

Nature with One Meaning

Nature plans the spring
of our lives transcribing
the dreams of its adolescence.
Flowers with little difference
in colors when they bloom
they stir and announce
their polite descend to the garden
or the roughness of wild verdure.
Winds traverse the plains
hair is blown by the wind
breasts open to the sunlight
suddenly marks from kisses vanish.
Spring close to the beginning
greenery, honeybees
the voice of cosmos is always youngish.
Yet what a monotony, what boredom
all this unbearable light of life
that you'll never see its end
and the more it reoccurs
the more you're grateful to it.
Yet the west
has so much variety.
You imagine each soul in a certain way
and it appears at the wrong time
always differently dressed and
always transmitting something mysterious.
The purple clouds fool you
and when they turn black
you think that you alone imagine them
you alone capture quite poetically
another utopia.
In final analysis the end is such
that it doesn't know the monotony
of existence
nor the recurrence
of the I.

Stowaway in a Dream

I appeared there, I sprouted
though no one ever saw me
I felt impatient
though I had nothing
to long for.
Darkness had dried up
inside me
and I had nothing to use
to nurture my dream
that used darkness
to illuminate the light
of life.
Only a neutral color
covered the stone of
my heart.
And behold, it came
after so long
with no imaginary joys
or excessive sorrow
the dream came
and it held only one purse:
my purse.

I had forgotten of it
I had looked for it
but without the sovereign
master of my present,
my panic,
yet with the serenity of a fairy tale.
I hadn't paid any ticket
but the dream
graced me quite graciously
with a short voyage
in a liberated country.
Liberated from the forceful
oversights of reality.

The Causality of Tears

Before the soul discovered
the tear, did nature exist
or the soul? What did it do
to express the absolute loss,
the loss of future time when
the *will* weakens and the horizon fogs
outside the open window?

Instead nature or the soul
cunningly invented the tear.
Pain gets freshened by it
wonder is watered
and produces fruit
while new questions
with substance
arise in the mind.

I wonder why, when, what we consider
important moves forward
in reality and we get closer
to the unshakable nothing.

The nothing
that we'll never face
and the flesh of the void
we'll never touch.
That barren nothing
which dries up the tears.

Season of Antipathy

The enemy of compassion
antipathy opposes passion
and spreads like a plague.

I loved all the animals
that tamed me, which
now creep like serpents
fixated as if preying and
with goggling eyes
they send me a message
that what is alive
isn't always the best
and what dies
isn't always despair.

Men with provocative pants
fabric stretched with imaginative
intention
men almost unshaven
with their cunning glances
disguised into animalistic fervor
that spreads thickly
on white bed-sheets
sink
in the moldy waters of memory
leaving behind them
not a shred of compassion
nor a bit of awe
for their conquests.

And women the so called friends
with whom I knit the web of life
and we laughed with each
crooked passing of the needle
and our confidential secrets
were told by our shining lips
we, who felt deep in our viscera
the importance of our existence on earth
even when the *one* would just
close the door behind him,
we became the bored ladies,
the stressed, manic housewives
with the desperate movements
who run to just catch the last train
of fame.

But the most distaste you feel
for the one
who feels all these
as if he is a superior being
as if he has wings
and flies over the dead
over ambitions and thrash
as if he is
your own self
less useless and disliked.

Total Destruction of the Ego

…and instead of despairing
for your ravaged skin
drowning in the deluge of *his* memory
as you face in distress
the barren field of your future,
while you often mention the word *tomorrow* out of habit
instead of the internal end of the world
the egoistic hope
that some meaning may hide in your life,
you feel an unexpected strong pain
seeing images of nature's destruction
the one which, in reality, was
the consolation of your soul
that you would live forever under the roots of its children
that you would feel leaves stirring under the soil
and that birds would perch on branches and rest for a moment.

Yet the horror before the darkest destruction
that encircles the forests
the horror you feel when you listen
to the predictions of the useless experts
that perhaps the tree tops
will never caress the sky on these mountain peaks
the horror strangely mixes with elation
in the roots of your heart
that you finally escaped from the prison of *ego*
which often with meaningless details
annulled your share of compassion.
You don't hang from the railings
of your unimportance anymore
you compare it to the eternal meaning
of germination
and you bestow your body unto it.

Life Saving Details

The immune system of my life
presents strange mutations
and what I always hated,
the attachment to detail,
helps me survive.
The repetition of a little movement,
of an idea, of a moment
grants me the courage to face
the sea of my life
that I can't traverse
the black curtain of the unknown
that is lowered in front of me.
Then go ahead, pick up the little garbage, I say
and forget the mountain of thrash
that piles up all around you.

Reminders of Eros

If Eros has forsaken you
you will remember of it
soon as you glance nature:
the mountain slopes, the waves
the deciduous trees
that never doubt the seasons
the animals which as soon as
they are born they know how to live,
how to defend themselves against enemies
as nature has provided for them.
Careful though that your renewed memory
runs to the pile of your betrayed
expectations, your unrealized dreams.

Poetic Postscript

Poems can't be beautiful
when truth has turned ugly.
Experience is the only
body of the poems now
and as experience is enriched
the poem finds nourishment
and becomes strong.
My knees hurt and I can't
kneel before poetry anymore
I can only gift it with
my experienced wounds.
The adjectives wilted
I can only use my imagination
to embellish poetry.
Yet I shall always serve it
as long as it too wishes
because only poetry makes me forget
the enclosed horizon of my future.

The Poet

Katerina Anghelaki-Rooke was born in Athens, February 1939. Nikos Kazantzakis, a good family friend, was her god-father. At the age of only 17 she wrote the poem *Loneliness* which her Nikos Kazantzakis forwarded to the editor of literary magazine New Epoch with the following note "please publish this poem; it was written by a 17 year old girl and it is the best poem I have ever read." Since that day her devotion to poetry and translation took wings. As herself pointed out in one of her interviews this was her entrance through the door of poetry.

She studied foreign languages and literature at the universities of Athens, Nice (France) and Geneva (Switzerland), where she was graduated in 1962. She has received Ford Foundation Grants (1972 and 1975), was invited to the International Writing Program at the University of Iowa, and was a Fulbright Visiting Lecturer in the United States (1980-1981), during which time she lectured on Modern Greek Poetry and Nikos Kazantzakis at Harvard. She has subsequently lectured on other dimensions of modern poetry and given public reading of her poetry in English and in Greek in the United States, Mexico, and Europe. She won the 1985 Greek National Poetry Award for the Greek version of *Beings and Things on Their Own*.

Her work has been translated into more than ten languages and is included in numerous anthologies. She has translated from English and French as well as from the Russian works of Shakespeare, Mayakovski, and Pushkin.

She's the recipient of the first poetry award Prix Hensch of the City of Geneva, the National Literary Award of Greece, the Kostas Ouranis poetry Award and in 2014 she was awarded the National Poetry Award for the whole of her literary accomplishment.

BIBLIOGRAPHY

LE GRAND GUIDE DE LA GRECE, Translated Dominique Saran, Gallimard, 1996
ENANTIOS EROTAS, Translated Ingemar Rhedin, Axion edition, 2005
LES RUSES D'ULYSSE, Inventaire, 2004
ENTRE CIEL ET TERRE, Eugène Van Itterbeek, Editions Les Sept Dormants, 1997
KDYZ KONCI DEN, I V SE STMIVA, Festival spisovatelů Praha, 2008
DANS LRE CIEL DU NEANT, Translated Michel Volkovitch, Editions Al Manar, "Voix vives de la Méditerranée", 2012.
BEINGS AND THINGS ON THEIR OWN, tr. K. Anghelaki-Rooke & J. Willcox (1986).
TRANSLATING INTO LOVE LIFE'S END, Shortstring Press.
THE SCATTERED PAPERS OF PENELOPE: NEW AND SELECTED POEMS, Graywolf Press.

The Translator

Emmanuel Aligizakis, (Manolis) is a Cretan-Canadian poet and author. He's the most prolific writer-poet of the Greek diaspora with 70 books published in more than a dozen different countries and in eleven different languages. At the age of eleven he transcribed the nearly 500 year old romantic poem Erotokritos, now released in a limited edition of 100 numbered copies and made available for collectors of such rare books at 5,000 dollars Canadian: the most expensive book of its kind to this day.

He was recently appointed an honorary instructor and fellow of the International Arts Academy, and awarded a Master's for the Arts in Literature. He is recognized for his ability to convey images and thoughts in a rich and evocative way that tugs at something deep within the reader. Born in the village of Kolibari on the island of Crete in 1947, he moved with his family at a young age to Thessaloniki and then to Athens, where he received his Bachelor of Arts in Political Sciences from the Panteion University of Athens.

After graduation, he served in the armed forces for two years and emigrated to Vancouver in 1973, where he worked as an iron worker, train labourer, taxi driver, and stock broker, and studied English Literature at Simon Fraser University. He has written three novels and numerous collections of poetry, which are steadily being released as published works.

His articles, poems and short stories in both Greek and English have appeared in various magazines and newspapers in Canada, United

States, Hungary, Slovakia, Romania, Australia, Jordan, Serbia and Greece. His poetry has been translated in Romanian, Swedish, German, Hungarian, Ukrainian, French, Portuguese, Arabic, Turkish, Serbian, Russian, Italian, Chinese, Japanese, languages and has been published in book form or in magazines in various countries.

He now lives in White Rock, where he spends his time writing, gardening, traveling, and heading Libros Libertad, an unorthodox and independent publishing company which he founded in 2006 with the mission of publishing literary books.

His translation book "George Seferis-Collected Poems" was shortlisted for the Greek National Literary Awards the highest literary recognition of Greece. In September 2017 he was awarded the First Poetry Prize of the Mihai Eminescu International Poetry Festival, in Craiova, Romania.

AWARDS

~1st Poetry Prize, Academy of Mihai Eminescu, Craiova, Romania, 2017
~Distinguished Poet and Writer Award, City of Richmond, BC, 2014
~1st Poetry Prize, International Arts Academy for this translation of "Yannis Ritsos- Selected Poems", 2014
~Winner of the Dr. Asha Bhargava Memorial Award, Writers International Network Canada, 2014
~"George Seferis-Collected Poems" translated by Manolis, shortlisted for the Greek National Literary Awards, translation category.
~1st Poetry Prize, International Arts Academy, for his translation of "George Seferis-Collected Poems", 2013
~Master of the Arts in Literature, International Arts Academy, 2013
~1st Prize for poetry, 7th Volos poetry Competition, 2012
~Honorary instructor and fellow, International Arts Academy, 2012
~2nd Prize for short story, Interartia festival, 2012
~2nd Prize for Poetry, Interartia Festival, 2012
~2nd Prize for poetry, Interartia Festival, 2011
~3rd Prize for short stories, Interartia Festival, 2011

BOOKS by MANOLIS ALIGIZAKIS

RED IN BLACK, poetry, Ekstasis Editions, 2019
THE QUEST, novel, Ekstasis Editions, 2018
THE MEDUSA GLANCE, poetry, Ekstasis Editions, spring 2017
THE SECOND ADVENT OF ZEUS, poetry, Ekstasis Editions, spring 2016
CHTHONIAN BODIES, paintings by Ken Kirkby and poems by Manolis Aligizakis, Libros Libertad, 2015
IMAGES OF ABSENCE, poetry, Ekstasis Editions, 2015
AUTUMN LEAVES, poetry, Ekstasis Editions, 2014
ÜBERMENSCH/ΥΠΕΡΑΝΘΡΩΠΟΣ, poetry, Ekstasis Editions, 2013
MYTHOGRAPHY, paintings and poems, Libros Libertad, 2012
NOSTOS AND ALGOS, poetry, Ekstasis Editions, 2012
VORTEX, poetry, Libros Libertad, 2011
THE CIRCLE, novel, Libros Libertad, 2011
VERNAL EQUINOX, poetry, Ekstasis Editions, 2011
OPERA BUFA, poetry, Libros Libertad, 2010
VESPERS, paintings and poems, Libros Libertad, 2010
TRIPTYCH, poetry, Ekstasis Editions, 2010
NUANCES, poetry, Ekstasis Editions, 2009
RENDITION, poetry, Libros Libertad, 2009
IMPULSES, poetry, Libros Libertad, 2009
TROGLODYTES, poetry, Libros Libertad, 2008
PETROS SPATHIS, novel, Libros Libertad, 2008
EL GRECO, poetry, Libros Libertad, 2007
PATH OF THORNS, poetry, Libros Libertad, 2006
FOOTPRINTS IN SANDSTONE, poetry, Authorhouse, Bloomington, Indiana, 2006
THE ORPHANS, poetry, Authorhouse, Bloomington, Indiana, 2005

TRANSLATIONS FROM GREEK TO ENGLISH

NEO-HELLENE POETS an ANTHOLOGY of MODERN GREEK POETRY 1750-2018, poetry translated by Manolis Aligizakis, Ekstasis Editions and Libros Libertad, 2018
KARYOTAKIS—POLYDOURI, The Tragic Love Story, poetry

translated by Manolis Aligizakis, Libros Libertad, 2016
HOURS OF THE STARS, poetry by Dimitris Liantinis, translated by Manolis Aligizakis, Libros Libertad, 2015
HEAR ME OUT, short stories, by Tzoutzi Mantzourani, translated by Manolis Aligizakis, Libros Libertad, 2015
CARESSING MYTHS, poetry by Dina Georgantopoulos, translated by Manolis Aligizakis, Libros libertad, 2015
IDOLATERS, a novel by Joanna Frangia, translated by Manolis Aligizakis, Libros Libertad, 2014
TASOS LIVADITIS-SELECTED POEMS, translated by Manolis Aligizakis, Libros Libertad, 2014
YANNIS RITSOS-SELECTED POEMS, translated by Manolis Aligizakis, Ekstasis Editions, 2013
CLOE AND ALEXANDRA-SELECTED POEMS, translated by Manolis Aligizakis, Libros Libertad, 2013
GEORGE SEFERIS-COLLECTED POEMS, translated by Manolis Aligizakis, Libros Libertad, 2012
YANNIS RITSOS-POEMS, translated by Manolis Aligizakis, Libros Libertad, 2010
CONSTANTINE P CAVAFY-POEMS, translated by Manolis Aligizakis, Libros Libertad, 2008
CAVAFY-SELECTED POEMS, translated by Manolis Aligizakis, Ekstasis Editions, 2011

TRANSLATIONS FROM ENGLISH TO GREEK

DIVINE KISS, poetry by Carolyn Mary Kleefeld, translated by Manolis Aligizakis, CCC Communications-Libros Libertad Publishing, 2018
LIGHT IN THE PINENEEDLES, poetry by Karoly Fellinger, translated from English to Greek by Manolis Aligizakis, OSTRIA Publications, Athens, Greece, 2017

BOOKS in OTHER LANGUAGES

NOSTOS ET ALGOS (French), poetry by Manolis Aligizakis

translated by Karoly Sandor Pallai, Ekstasis Editions, 2019.
MEDUSA BAKISI (THE MEDUSA GLANCE in Turkish) poetry by Mnaolis Aligizakis translated by Pelin Batu, Artshop Publishing, Istanbul, 2019
SECOND ADVENT OF ZEUS, (Portuguese) poetry by Manolis Aligizakis, translated in Portuguese by Eric Ponty, Musa Editora, Sao Paolo, Brazil, 2018
ODE TO APHRODITE, (Arabic), poetry by Manolis Aligizakis, translated in Arabic by Fethi Sassi, Borsa Publishing, Cairo, Egypt, 2018
THORNS OF THE ROSE, (Romanian), poetry by Manolis Aligizakis, translated in Romanian by Tatjana Betoska, Editura Europa, Craiova, Romania, 2017.
FOGOLY, (Hungarian) novel by Manolis, translated in Hungarian by Karoly Csiby, Parnassus Publications, Bratislava, Hungary, 2017
FUILLES D'AUTOMNE, poetry by Manolis Aligizakis, translated into French by Karoly Sandor Pallai, Editions Du Cygne, Paris, 2017
NABORI SEĆANJA, (Serbian) poetry by Manolis Aligizakis, translated into Serbian by Jolanka Kovacs, Zrenjanin, Serbia, 2016
FRUNZE DE TOAMNA, Poetry by Manolis, translated by Lucia Gorea, AB-ART, Romania, 2016
OSZI FALEVELEK, (Hungarian), poetry by Manolis Aligizakis, translated into Hungarian by Karoly Csiby, Gyp, Hungary, 2015
SVEST, (Serbian), poetry by Manolis Aligizakis, translated into Serbian by Jolanka Kovacs, Serbia, 2015
ESZMELET, (Hungarian), poetry by Manolis Aligizakis, translated into Hungarian by Karoly Csiby, AB-ART, Bratislava, Slovakia, 2014
ÜBERMENSCH (German), poetry by Manolis Aligizakis, translated into German by Eniko Thiele Csekei, WINDROSE, Austria, 2014
NOSTOS SI ALGOS, (Romanian) poetry by Manolis Aligizakis, translated into Romanian by Lucia Gorea, DELLART, Cluj-Napoca, Romania, 2013

BOOKS IN GREEK

IN THE WIRLPOOL OF STOCK EXCHANGE, novel (Greek)

OSTRIA Publications, Athens, Greece, 2019

PAINTINGS and TRANSCENDENCES, (Greek) poetry by Manolis Aligizakis, paintings by Ken Kirkby, OSTRIA Publications, Athens, 2019

THE CIRCLE, novel, (Greek) Korontzis Publicatios, Athens, 2018

NOTES OF A WET AUGUST, poetry, (Greek), Korontzis Publications, Athens, 2018

THE PRISONER, novel, (Greek), OSTRIA Publications, Athens, Greece, 2017

BLUE IN THE WINDOW poetry, (Greek) OSTRIA Publications, Athens, Greece, 2017

SECOND ADVENT OF ZEUS, pooetry, (Greek), ENEKEN Publications, Thessaloniki, Greece, spring 2017

MEMORIES, poetry, (Greek) Fildisi Editions, Athens, Greece, 2016

SONGS OF THE ABSURD, poetry, (Greek) ENEKEN, Salonika, Greece, 2015

IMAGES OF ABSENCE, poetry, (Greek), Sexpirikon, Salonika, Greece, 2015

HIERODULES, poetry, (Greek), Sexpirikon, Salonika, Greece, 2014

YPERANTHROPOS, poetry, (Greek) ENEKEN, Salonika, Greece, 2014

TOLMIRES ANATASEIS, poetry, (Greek), GAVRIILIDIS EDITIONS, Athens, Greece, 2013

FYLLOROES, poetry, (Greek) ENEKEN PUBLICATIONS, Salonika, Greece, 2013

EARINI ISIMERIA, poetry, (Greek) ENEKEN PUBLICATIONS, Salonika, Greece, 2011

STRATIS ROUKOUNAS, novel, (Greek), MAVRIDIS EDITIONS, Athens, Greece, 1981

LONGHAND BOOKS

EROTOKRITOS, by Vitsentzos Kornaros, (rare book-collectible), transcribed by Manolis Aligizakis, Libros Libertad, 2015

www.ingramcontent.com/pod-product-compliance
Lightning Source LLC
Chambersburg PA
CBHW070449050426
42451CB00015B/3401